POTTERIES MOTOR TRACTION

CLIFF BEETON

AMBERLEY

First published 2021

Amberley Publishing
The Hill, Stroud
Gloucestershire, GL5 4EP

www.amberley-books.com

Copyright © Cliff Beeton, 2021

The right of Cliff Beeton to be identified as
the Author of this work has been asserted in
accordance with the Copyrights, Designs and
Patents Act 1988.

ISBN 978 1 3981 0866 0 (print)
ISBN 978 1 3981 0867 7 (ebook)

British Library Cataloguing in Publication Data.
A catalogue record for this book is available from
the British Library.

Origination by Amberley Publishing.
Printed in the UK.

Introduction

We start this book at the beginning of the 1980s when Potteries Motor Traction (PMT) was part of the state-owned National Bus Company (NBC) and the majority of its fleet was painted in the standard poppy red livery with a white relief band. The last pre-NBC buses had recently left the fleet following service reductions, with the implementation of the NBC's 'Market Analysis Project'. The double-deck fleet now consisted of Eastern Coach Works (ECW) bodied Bristol VRTs and their recent successors, the ECW-bodied Leyland Olympians; however, two unique trial buses delivered in 1977, an Alexander-bodied Dennis Dominator and a Northern Counties-bodied Foden NC, continued to add a bit of variety to the fleet .The single-deck fleet contained both long and short versions of the ECW-bodied Bristol RE and subsequent Leyland National, along with Leyland Leopard dual-purpose coaches. These were later joined by a batch of six Leyland National 2s and the Leopards' replacement, the Leyland Tiger.

Rumours of the imminent failure of Berresfords Motors and its Stoniers subsidiary in 1983 saw ten Bristol Omnibus Company RELLs arrive from Bristol to cover these services. They ran in service in the Potteries in green livery with PMT fleet names, but Berresfords kept going so the majority had departed the fleet within a year.

Government policy to sell off the National Bus Company alongside the deregulation of the bus services themselves, would see the introduction of a new red and yellow livery in 1985 as a prelude to the management buyout in 1986.

Following the management buyout, PMT expanded outside their traditional area into Stockport, Moreton, Wolverhampton and Leeds by running tendered services under the Red Rider fleet name. The Leeds operations were renamed Cityline after a legal challenge from Yorkshire Rider. An outstation was also opened at Crewe to service the work won from Crosville in that town.

Acquisitions would see local independents Berresfords, Stoniers and Turner's join the fold in 1987, with Pennine Blue of Denton joining in 1990. In 1990, PMT acquired the Chester and Wirral operations of Crosville from Drawlane. The bus services of Poole's Coachways of Alsagers Bank would also be acquired.

New buses flooded into the fleet, with ten Leyland Olympians in 1989 followed by nine Optare Deltas and eleven Leyland Lynxes in 1990 before the Dennis Dart midibus became the new standard. All had dual-purpose seating. Minibuses also arrived in large numbers. The bus operations of Topp-Line, Liverpool, along with four Leyland Lynxes, were acquired in 1994.

In 1994, PMT was purchased by the Badgerline Group and from then on took delivery of Badgerline standard vehicles, including Plaxton Verde and Northern Counties-bodied Dennis Lances and Plaxton Pointer Dennis Darts. These vehicles were subsequently delivered with standard bus seating.

In 1996, Badgerline merged with GRT to form First Bus, which initially allowed PMT to keep the red and yellow livery, but this changed in 1997 when the group's standard livery was introduced. This would see the end of intergroup transfers running in their old liveries in the

Potteries. It would also see the end of the Turner's of Brown Edge livery, which was kept for buses working the former Turner's route.

Rationalisation would see the depots at Leeds closed and the Wolverhampton depot was sold to Stevensons of Uttoxeter in exchange for its Pacer operations in Stockport, which were merged with the Red Rider operation to form an enlarged Pennine operation. The Red Rider operations on the Wirral were merged with the Crosville ones. The Crewe depot finally closed as new local independent operators gradually took over the tenders the depot worked.

Garage closures in the Potteries saw Hanley, Cheadle, Burslem and Newcastle all closed, with all operations centred on the new garage at Adderley Green. Further rationalisation would see the Pennine operations transfer to First Manchester in April 2001, although many buses had received the First Manchester orange livery ahead of the transfer.

The Crosville operations in Chester would be expanded with the purchase of Chester City Transport in June 2007, but these would also transfer to First Manchester in September 2010 and would later be sold to Stagecoach in 2013.

First Potteries, as PMT had become, now has just the one garage at Adderley Green, and its area of operation is now centred on the Potteries, with Stafford, Leek, Uttoxeter, and Crewe being the only towns outside the Stoke-on-Trent area now served.

On the livery side of things, the relaxation of the rigid First Bus livery saw two different livery schemes started but never completed. The former red and yellow livery was reactivated for Gold Service Routes 25 and 26, but abandoned after just four repaints. The later different-coloured front scheme was abandoned after red, mauve and turquoise when the raspberry front scheme for Route 6, Hanley–Meir–Blythe Bridge, was renamed fuchsia and adopted as the company standard. The latest livery, introduced at the end of 2019, has different coloured buses for specific routes: the Leek Link is green for the No. 18, Hanley–Leek; the Knotty purple for the No. 101, Hanley–Stafford; and the Kingfisher turquoise for the KF, Hanley–Uttoxeter; however, the Covid-19 pandemic sees these appearing on any route as required.

At the end of 2020, surplus 2006-registered Wright Eclipse-bodied Volvo B7RLE buses started to be returned to First Group following their hire to Diamond Bus after the sale of First Manchester's Bolton depot. Sixteen of these buses were allocated to First Potteries to start replacing the slightly older Alexander Dennis Enviro 300s in the fleet.

I have tried to show as many examples of different vehicles and liveries as possible, starting with poppy red, the green REs, the all-over advert era, the privatised red and yellow era (with associated variants like the Bradwell and Silverdale shuttles, Crosville, Red Rider and Turner's of Brown Edge), then the later standard Barbie liveries, various coloured fronts, the latest livery offerings, buses in former operator's liveries, demonstrators and hire-ins, and even a couple of unfortunate fire victims. Enjoy!

PMT took delivery of its first ECW-bodied Bristol VRTs in 1974, with some of these initially going on loan to Crosville in Liverpool in green livery. REH 817M (No. 617) was an early example and was still looking smart eight years later when arriving at Hanley bus station. Early examples had grey window rubbers and later examples would have black.

PMT took delivery of a total of 131 new ECW-bodied Bristol VRTs between 1974 and 1980 during the time that it was the National Bus Company standard double-decker. The final one to be delivered was NEH 732W (No. 732), seen in Hanley on an afternoon trip to Keele. Additional second-hand VRTs would later join the fleet after privatisation.

The last double-deckers delivered new to PMT in 1983 under National Bus Company ownership were fifteen ECW-bodied Leyland Olympians, which had replaced the now discontinued Bristol VRT and subsequently became the NBC standard double-decker. The last one to be delivered was A747 JRE (No. 747), seen here in Burslem in NBC poppy red livery when still relatively new.

The first Bristol VRT to be withdrawn, although somewhat prematurely, was HRE 528N (No. 628), which met its fate in early 1982 when only seven years old after catching fire and being badly damaged. The remains are seen at the rear of the old Stoke garage in Woodhouse Street awaiting removal for scrap.

A unique bus in the PMT fleet was low-height, Northern Counties-bodied Foden NC WVT 900S (No. 900), one of two trial buses that entered the PMT fleet in 1978 for comparison trials against the standard Bristol VRT. It proved troublesome in service and was frequently off the road awaiting parts. It is seen here leaving Newcastle garage on a No. 364 route for Market Drayton in 1982.

The other trial bus in the PMT fleet was low-height, Alexander-bodied Dennis Dominator XBF 700S (No. 700), seen here reversing off the stand at the old Newcastle bus station in 1982 shortly before being transferred to fellow NBC subsidiary Maidstone & District, who operated similar buses but with highbridge bodywork.

The 11.5-metre-long Leyland National was the most numerous in the PMT fleet, with thirty-nine examples delivered new to the company between 1972 and 1977. They looked their best in poppy red livery with a white relief band, such as KRE 280P (No. 280) parked outside the old Newcastle garage.

PMT also took delivery of fifteen short, 10.5-metre Leyland Nationals in 1973–74, such as XEH 258M (No. 258) seen here arriving at the old Longton bus station in the short-lived all-over poppy red livery without the white relief band – a National Bus Company policy to save money. Unlike the longer examples they had short lives with the company, with most lasting less than ten years.

After withdrawal from the main fleet Alexander-bodied Daimler Fleetline AEH 135C (No. 1035) was transferred to the driver training school and repainted into the training bus yellow and white livery. It is seen here parked up on the wasteland adjacent to the former Stoke garage and main works in Woodhouse Street.

PMT acquired twelve Bristol RELL buses with ECW bodywork from Bristol Omnibus in 1983 – ten for further service and two for spares. As they were due to stay in the fleet for a short time they entered service in leaf green livery, but with PMT fleet names on the front to assure passengers they were PMT buses. OHU769F (No. 174) still carries its Bristol-cast numberplate when seen at Newcastle.

All the leaf green ECW-bodied Bristol RELLs from Bristol carried the early flat-fronted ECW bodywork apart from one: EHU 379K (No. 180), which carried the later curved windscreen as seen here leaving Hanley for Crewe on a No. 320. Despite being the newest of the new arrivals, it didn't last the longest.

The majority of PMT's ECW-bodied Bristol RESLs were withdrawn after the Market Analysis Project exercises in the early 1980s when still relatively new. Only two managed to survive this cull. One being PVT 204L (No. 204), as seen here at the old Newcastle garage. The other survivor was PVT 207L (No. 207).

Six dual-purpose Leyland National 2 buses were the last full-sized, single-deck buses delivered to PMT under National Bus Company ownership, but they had relatively short lives with the company. A304 JFA (No. 304) is seen leaving Hanley in its red and white dual-purpose livery on a No. 239 to Alton. This bus was later sold to Nip On Buses, St Helens, for further service.

PMT only ever operated three of the ECW dual-purpose, bus-bodied Bristol RELH buses with coach seats designed for the longer distance interurban routes. One of these was MVT 211K (No. 211), seen here in the red and white dual-purpose livery loading on a No. 249 to Hilderstone outside Hanley bus station.

Some of PMT's Leyland Nationals were outshopped in the rather drab all-over poppy red livery without the white relief band – apparently to save money. One such example was GBF 71N (No. 268), seen here outside the old Longton bus station. It carries a Potteries fleet name as opposed to a PMT one.

Former Bristol Omnibus ECW-bodied Bristol RELL OHW 535F (No. 175) was one of only two of the batch of ten that operated in green livery with PMT fleet names to survive long enough to receive a coat of poppy red. It is seen here at Burslem shortly after its repaint. It would later be renumbered '205'.

PVT 227L (No. 227) was one of the few PMT ECW-bodied Bristol RELLs to receive the all-over poppy red livery without the white relief band, a dubious National Bus Company edict to supposedly save money on repaints. It looks rather drab here, laying over in the old Hanley bus station on an equally drab winter's day.

PMT have only ever operated two ECW-bodied Bristol LHS buses. They arrived from National Welsh during the final months of National Bus Company ownership, but their use was rather patchy – probably due to their unfamiliar manual gearboxes. GTX 762W (No. 311) looks smart in the NBC red and white dual-purpose livery when seen here at Newcastle.

Duple Dominant Express-bodied Leyland Leopard coach GRF 267V (No. 67) was delivered in dual-purpose red and white livery, but later received National Express white livery. It is seen here on normal service work at Crewe on a No. 323 to Hanley bus station. This vehicle would later see further service with Mayne of Manchester.

Plaxton Paramount-bodied, high-floor Leyland Tiger A26 JFA (No. 26) was used on the National Express Rapide Service 545 between Hanley and London Victoria coach station. It carried a host serving hot drinks and snacks during the journey. It is seen at the old Hanley garage being prepared for its next journey to London in 1983.

Duple Dominant Express-bodied Leyland Leopard coach XBF 54S (No. 54) wears the National Bus Company dual-purpose red and white livery when seen here laying over in the old Hanley bus station. It would go on to receive the later red and yellow livery before being sold for further service to Camms Coaches of Nottingham.

The other ECW-bodied Bristol LH to arrive in the PMT fleet from National Welsh was GTX 760W (No. 310). This initially received National Express white striped livery with Paramount fleet names as seen here at the old Hanley garage, but would later be repainted into blue and yellow for the K12 Coppenhall Clipper service at Crewe.

The all-over advertisement bus was very popular in the 1980s, and a very colourful example was ECW-bodied Bristol VRT NEW 724W (No. 724) advertising the virtues of BBC Radio Stoke and DJ Bruno Brookes. It is seen here at Shelton on a No. 24 to Meir Square with the now demolished Unity House towering behind it.

A much more sedate all-over advert bus was ECW-bodied Bristol VRT MFA 723V (No. 723), which carried this turquoise-based livery for the National Travelworld travel agency. It is seen parked on the forecourt of the now demolished Burslem garage in NBC days.

ECW-bodied Bristol VRT NEH 731W (No. 731) managed to receive a record three different all-over adverts between carrying poppy red and receiving a repaint into the red and yellow livery. It is seen at Goldenhill carrying a white, yellow and blue scheme to promote PMT's in-house Buzzabout travelcard.

ECW-bodied Bristol VRT NEH 729W (No. 729) received this blue and white all-over advert livery for NFC car auctions. It is seen in Charles Street, Hanley, working a No. 68 to the large Bentilee housing estate. Whether you love them or hate them they are definitely eye-catching, and were all hand-painted too – no vinyl wraps in those days.

Three Leyland Leopard coaches with Willowbrook bodywork arrived in 1982 in the standard National Bus Company dual-purpose red and white livery. VFA 71X (No. 71), seen here at the old Hanley garage, has been recently repainted into National Express white livery; however, it still didn't last long in the fleet and it later passed to OK Motor Services, Bishop Auckland, for further services.

XEH 252M (No. 252) was the only short, 10.5-metre Leyland National to last long enough to receive the red and yellow livery in September 1985, being the first single-decker to be painted red and yellow. It is seen here adjacent to the old Stoke garage after emerging from the paint shop. It lasted just over two years in this scheme before being repainted into Turner's of Brown Edge brown and cream livery.

The first double-decker to appear in the new red and yellow livery was PEH 653R (No. 653). It is seen at Newcastle bus station shortly after the repaint, complete with the NBC double 'N' symbol. It has red wheels and the internal panels behind the driver and on the platform are painted a buff colour – things that were not continued on subsequent repaints.

All fifteen of the ECW-bodied Leyland Olympians received the red and yellow livery, so didn't last too long in the original poppy red scheme that they were delivered new in a few years earlier. A737 GFA (No. 737) is seen resting at the old Newcastle garage.

Only one of the three ECW dual-purpose-bodied Bristol RELH buses ever received the red and yellow livery: MVT 211K (No. 211), which is seen in Charles Street, Hanley, on a No. 232 to Tean. These buses tended to operate on the longer-distance interurban services.

Many of the 11.5-metre Leyland Nationals survived long enough to receive red and yellow livery. PVT 244L (No. 244) was one such and is seen at Congleton bus station working a No. 312 to Hanley, still looking smart despite being fourteen years old. Today PMT buses no longer serve Congleton.

Many of the ECW-bodied Bristol RELLs received the red and yellow livery and tended to work on tendered services outside the Potteries area. PVT 220L (No. 220) is seen leaving Crewe on a K16 to Elm Drive. PMT managed to win a lot of tendered work after deregulation around Crewe that was previously worked by Crosville, and they opened a depot in the town to service that work.

Of the batch of second-hand Bristol REs from Bristol that ran initially in green livery, only two lasted long enough to receive the NBC poppy red; however, OHU 766F (No. 205) went one better and even managed to receive the red and yellow livery. It is seen in Tunstall working a No. 312 from Congleton to Hanley. The pottery works behind the bus is now an Asda supermarket.

Leyland National 2 A305 JFA (No. 305) was an early recipient of the new red and yellow livery, and as it was applied during National Bus Company days it received the NBC double 'N' symbol on the front too. It is seen at the old Hanley garage with blinds set for the short-lived X41 Hanley–Leicester via Burton-on-Trent service.

Two Mark 1 Leyland Nationals received this pale blue and yellow version of the standard livery, with Silverdale Shuttle branding for the Newcastle–Silverdale route formerly operated by Poole's Coachways. KRE 278P (No. 278) is seen here outside the old Hanley garage on a journey to Hanley. KRE 279P (No. 279) was the other National to receive this livery.

Leyland National 2 A303 JFA (No. 303), along with A301 JFA (No. 301), was one of two vehicles that received this mid-blue and yellow version of the standard livery with Bradwell Shuttle branding for Route 30, Hanley–Newcastle–Bradwell. It is seen here in Merrial Street, Newcastle, heading for Bradwell.

Two ECW-bodied Leyland Olympians, Nos 734 and 736, received a variation of the red and yellow livery, with the red being replaced with dark blue and branding for Route 17, Hanley–Bradwell. A734 GFA (No. 734) is seen at Church Lawton working a peak-hour timetabled journey on Route 321 to Alsager.

Accidents do happen. Bristol VRT YBF 687S (No. 687) had only just been repainted from poppy red into the red and yellow livery when it came to grief after catching fire at Ladderedge, near Leek. It is seen here after the fire brigade had just left, but before the recovery vehicle had arrived. Thankfully, nobody was hurt.

Plaxton Paramount-bodied Leyland Tiger ERF 24Y (No. 24) was originally a front-line coach for National Express work, but was later repainted into the red and yellow livery and lettered up for the X64 Hanley–Shrewsbury route – a joint service at the time with Midland Red North. It would later transfer to the Crosville operation on the Wirral.

Following the purchase of Stoniers of Goldenhill and Berresfords of Cheddleton in 1987, the Stoniers vehicles at the Tunstall garage were washed and fuelled at PMT's Burslem garage for a few weeks before being withdrawn and the garage closed. Stoniers Alexander-bodied Daimler Fleetline NWA 265K (new to Sheffield Transport) is seen outside Burslem garage after a wash and refuel. It was withdrawn shortly afterwards.

The only vehicle acquired with the purchase of Berresfords of Cheddleton and Stoniers of Goldenhill to receive the red and yellow bus livery was ECW coach-bodied Bristol RELH PCH 418L (No. 203), seen here outside the former garage at Stoke. This vehicle was new to Trent Motor Traction. Some of the former coach fleets later received Paramount and National Express livery.

Shortly after the PMT takeover, former Turner's of Brown Edge Daimler Fleetline JBF 169N (No. 750) still carries its old fleet number – '10' – and has a conductor onboard as it reverses into Sandy Lane at Brown Edge before returning to Hanley. The only clue to the new ownership are the external adverts and notices on the windows.

Turner's Leyland Fleetline LVT 699V (No. 752) is seen parked outside the former Turner's garage at Brown Edge shortly after the takeover. It is still using manual setright ticketing and working from the Brown Edge garage. The only clue to PMT ownership is the legal lettering and window notices. The garage later closed, with the buses moving to PMT's Hanley garage at Clough Street.

The sole surviving short Leyland National XEH 252M (No. 252) received Turner's livery shortly after the acquisition of Turner's, and is seen shortly afterwards at Hanley garage fitted with one of the new combined destination displays designed for the Turner's Fleetlines. It had been many years since Turner's had operated single-deck buses, but they had run coaches right up to the sale.

The two Roe-bodied Leyland Olympians acquired with the Turner's operation received the more brown PMT version of the livery and, very rarely, managed to venture out onto other PMT routes; for example, EWY 78Y (No. 748) seen at Chesterton on a Sunday No. 434 from Audley–Hanley. Being higher than the standard PMT Olympians, they were soon transferred to the Red Rider operation at Stockport and painted red and yellow.

A740 GFA (No. 740), along with A742 GFA (No. 742), was one of two PMT ECW-bodied Leyland Olympians to receive Turner's livery following the sale of the three Turner's Fleetlines. This livery was more brown than the original Tudor maroon used by Turner's. It is seen here at the old Hanley garage.

PMT tried out many different demonstrators from different manufacturers before ordering twenty new single-deckers in 1990 for the busy Route 24, Meir Square–Talke Pits. Vehicles tried out were a Leyland Lynx, an Optare Delta, an Alexander-bodied Scania N113 and a Northern Counties-bodied Renault. Leyland Lynx E709 MFV is seen in Congleton on a No. 312 from Hanley.

The first purchase of new vehicles following the management buyout were ten all-Leyland Olympians in 1989, with six wearing a new silver, red and yellow livery for trunk route No. 320, Hanley–Crewe. G760 XRE (No. 760) is seen at Crewe bus station when new. These buses greatly increased the patronage on this route with their comfortable coach seating and impressive speed over previous offerings.

Following on from the Leyland Olympians the next major purchase of new vehicles by PMT following the management buyout from the National Bus Company were twenty single-deckers for trunk route No. 24, Meir Square–Talke Pits. Eleven of these were Leyland Lynxes, such as H859 GRE (No. 859) being delivered new to Newcastle garage for storage ahead of entry into service.

Along with the eleven Leyland Lynxes the other nine buses ordered were DAF SB220s with stylish Optare Delta bodywork. All twenty replaced Bristol VRTs at Burslem garage on the main-line Route 24, Meir Square–Talke Pits. H807 GRE (No. 807) is seen at the Meir Square terminus soon after entering service.

Following the purchase of the Crosville operations at Chester, Ellesmere Port and Birkenhead from Drawlane in 1990, a start was made repainting the fleet into the red and yellow fleet livery. Bristol VRT WTU 465W (No. DVG 465) is seen at Chester garage shortly afterwards receiving attention from the fitters. It is still in the Brunswick green and cream livery, but with PMT legal lettering.

After the purchase of the Crosville operations on the Wirral some former Crosville vehicles were transferred to the main PMT fleet for further service, with some working in full Crosville livery. One such transfer was Brislol VRT TMA 331R (DVL 331), seen here in Burslem working a No. 24 wearing the newer Drawlane Crosville livery with Town Lynx fleet names.

After the acquisition of the Crosville operations on the Wirral from Drawlane, the standard red and yellow livery began to be applied to the Crosville fleet, with a Crosville fleet name on the front despite initial thoughts of a green and yellow version. Here, Leyland Olympian B199 DTU (No. DOG 199) is seen at Birkenhead Woodside on a No. 71 to Heswall.

Following the purchase of the Crosville operations on the Wirral, some Crosville vehicles were repainted red and yellow and transferred to the main PMT fleet. One such vehicle was Duple Dominant-bodied Leyland Leopard coach JMB 336T (No. 2336), seen looking resplendent at the old Hanley Garage shortly after being repainted.

One of an assortment of different vehicles acquired with the Pennine Blue of Duckinfield operation was ECW-bodied Bristol RELL LTG 41L (No. 41), seen here at Duckinfield still carrying its former fleet number. It was new to Aberdare, later passing to Cynon Valley, and worked for many different operators before arriving at Pennine Blue, but didn't last long following the PMT takeover.

Following the acquisition of Pennine Blue at Duckinfield, some PMT Bristol VRTs were transferred to the Pennine Blue operation and painted in a blue and yellow version of standard livery to allow withdrawal of many of the older vehicles. BRF 693T (No. 1493) is seen at Duckinfield. This was short-lived, however, as the buses later received the standard red and yellow livery with just Pennine fleet names.

ECW-Bodied Leyland Olympian A740 GFA (No. DOG 740) carries the final double-deck version of Turner's livery with more cream and less brown, seen here at the old Hanley Garage shortly after repaint. It was one of a pair, along with A742 GFA (No. DOG 742), that operated the Hanley–Brown Edge–Endon route until the double-deckers were replaced by Dennis Darts.

After trying out demonstration vehicles from Chester and Rossendale at Newcastle garage, PMT ordered a batch of eighteen Dennis Darts in 1991 with Reeve Burgess Pointer bodywork. The first three were for the PMT operation at Newcastle and the other fifteen were for the Crosville operation on the Wirral. J914 SEH (No. MDC 914) is seen at Birkenhead Woodside.

Four of the second batch of Plaxton Pointer-bodied Dennis Darts, K926-9 XRF (Nos 926–929) carried a more yellow version of the standard red and yellow livery for the No. 260/X60 Hanley–Stafford route. K928 XRF (No. 928) is seen arriving in Hanley from Stafford when new. These buses were soon replaced on the Stafford route by larger vehicles.

All the initial batches of Dennis Darts carried the Reeve Burgess, and later Plaxton Pointer, bodywork, but two batches with Marshall bodywork entered service with Crosville on the Wirral and Pennine at Duckinfield. M949 SRE (No. 949) is seen with Crosville fleet names at Birkenhead Woodside.

The Plaxton Verde-bodied Dennis Lance was a Badgerline standard vehicle and five entered service in the PMT fleet at Burslem garage in 1995. Three received the standard red and yellow livery as seen on N865 CEH (No. SDC 865) at the Meir Square terminus of Route 24, a route they tended to work most of the time.

The final two Plaxton Verde-bodied Dennis Lances that entered service at Burslem garage in 1995 were painted in the interurban silver, red and yellow livery with branding for the No. 320 Crewe–Hanley. These replaced two of the coach-seated Leyland Olympians on that route. N867 CEH (No. SDC 867) is seen outside Burslem garage.

PMT took delivery of nine Leyland Swift midibuses with home-built PMT Knype bodywork. Initially having manual transmission, they were later converted to automatic, but being high floor they were not too successful on service work. G318 YVT (No. IWC 318) is seen leaving Hanley for Longton via Bentilee.

Former Crosville Leyland Olympian GFM 105X (No. 2105) was repainted red and yellow and transferred to the Red Rider operation at Wolverhampton. It is seen here at Wolverhampton bus station working a No. 545 to Bilston. The Wolverhampton operation was later sold to Stevensons of Uttoxeter in exchange for the Stevensons operations at Stockport.

A batch of seven second-hand Bristol VRs were acquired in 1989 from South Midland & Yorkshire Traction due to increases in tendered work. Ex-South Midland YBW 488V (No. 772) works a No. 24 to Talke Pits in full South Midland livery complete with cast numberplate '639'. After a repaint this bus was transferred to the Crewe outstation.

Another ex-South Midland Bristol VR acquired from Thames Transit was YBW 489V (No. 773), which entered service in the Potteries in full South Midland Orbiter livery complete with cast numberplate '640' working a No. 24 to Meir Square at Burslem before receiving a repaint into red and yellow.

National Express work ensured that new coaches continued to arrive into the fleet to operate these services. Plaxton Expressliner-bodied Volvo B10M-60 G118 XRE (No. 18) looks smart as it waits at the old Hanley garage to work a No. 830 to Oxford. This coach didn't last too long with PMT before passing on to Ribble for further service.

Four Leyland Lynx joined the Crosville fleet when PMT purchased the bus services of Topp-Line of Wavertree in 1994. They initially ran in the Topp-Line livery of orange, blue and white but with Crosville flee tnames and fleet numbers. F364 YTJ (No. SLC 848) is seen on layover at Birkenhead Woodside.

After the purchase of the Crosville operations on the Wirral some of the Crosville coach-seated, ECW-bodied Leyland Olympians received the interurban silver red and yellow livery as used on the Hanley–Crewe route, such as B200 DTU (No. DOG 896) seen leaving the old Chester Bus Exchange on the X8 for Southport.

Bristol VR OEH 605M (No. 605) was one of the few Bristol VRTs, apart from accident victims, never to receive the red and yellow livery. It went straight from NBC poppy red into training bus yellow livery after being adapted after withdrawal for use as a driver trainer. It is seen here parked up on the spare ground next to the old Stoke garage.

Bristol VR 507 EXA (No. 622) was originally registered 'GBF 78N' and was converted to open top for special events. It is seen here at the now closed Chatterley Whitfield mining museum during a bus rally held there in 1992. The bus was later transferred to First Devon and Cornwall for use between Penzance and Lands' End.

Inter-company transfers within First Group saw two Duple Dominant bus-bodied Volvo B10s arrive from First Capital, and these initially ran in service in the Potteries in their yellow livery. D499 NYS (No. 885), seen here at Newcastle-under-Lyme, had received a repaint into red and yellow. It was new to Hutchison of Overtown.

Three Leyland Olympians with Northern Counties lowheight bodywork arrived in the Potteries from Yorkshire Rider and looked very smart in the red and yellow livery. F156 XYG (No. 889) is seen at Newcastle-under-Lyme soon after arriving in the Potteries. These buses would later transfer to the Pennine operation at Duckinfield, as GMPTE tenders in Greater Manchester required more modern buses to be used.

More inter-company transfers saw second-hand East Lancs-bodied Dennis Dominators arrive for the Crosville fleet at Birkenhead from First Capital, which had been new to Leicester and Southampton. F298 PTP (No. 698) is seen during a visit to the Potteries at Newcastle garage.

Three of the 1989 batch of ten all-Leyland Olympians delivered new to PMT were fitted with bus seating, while the other seven had coach seats. G754 XRE (No. 754) and G755 XRE (No. 755) are seen together on the forecourt of the old Newcastle Garage when still fairly new.

An interesting arrival from Brewers but new to Eastern National was HHJ 374Y (No. STL 297), an Alexander TE-bodied Leyland Tiger for a school contract at Newcastle. It occasionally escaped onto service work, as seen here at Hanley. This bus later transferred to the Pennine operation at Duckinfield.

Ten eighty-four-seat Alexander RH-bodied tri-axle Leyland Olympians were imported from New World Firstbus in Hong Kong for the Pennine operation at Duckinfield to improve the age profile required on GMPTE tenders. They were delivered in the red and yellow livery but were soon repainted into the Barbie scheme. K486 EUX (No. 686) is seen at Duckinfield.

Another foreign import was SBS 7204J (No. 700) an ex-Singapore Alexander RH-bodied Volvo Olympian, which was originally to be the first of over a hundred to arrive from that source but was destined to be the only one. It received the registration 'K174 EUX' and is seen at Adderley Green with PMT fleet names but never worked in the Potteries, entering service at the Pennine operation at Duckinfield.

Two Leyland Olympians with Northern Counties bodywork were transferred to Pennine from First Manchester, repainted red and yellow and numbered 626–7. A658 HNB (No. 7627) is seen at the Duckinfield garage shortly before the transfer of the Pennine operation to First Manchester and carries temporary fleet number 7627. It would later regain its original First Manchester fleet number, 8658.

A batch of Optare Metroriders received the silver, red and yellow livery for Route B6, Biddulph–Hanley. R394 ERE (No. IPC 394) is just starting its journey to Hanley when seen on the Park Lane estate at Biddulph. The First Group standard Barbie scheme would see off all these interesting livery variations.

Following the success of the silver, red and yellow livery on the Leyland Olympians on the Crewe–Hanley route, a similar livery was applied to other vehicles operating on the longer routes. DAF SB220 H805 GRE (No. SAD 805) shows off the new livery at Sneyd Green when the No. 18 ran all the way from Leek to Keele.

Some of the early Plaxton Pointer-bodied Dennis Darts also received the silver livery, but these were always better suited to the shorter routes. K929 XRF (No. IDC 929), formerly in the No. 260 more yellow livery, is off route at Ball Green working a No. 46 to Blurton despite being branded up for the Keele–Hanley–Stafford route.

PMT celebrated its centenary in 1998 and repainted Leyland Lynx H856 GRE (No. SLC 856) into this red and cream livery that was carried by the early trams a century earlier. It is seen here looking immaculate leaving Burslem on a No. 24 for Hanley and Meir shortly after the repaint.

Turner's of Brown Edge had been very well respected by the public, so the livery continued in various forms under PMT ownership and was only finally phased out with the adoption of the First Group standard Barbie livery. Plaxton Pointer-bodied Dennis Dart L939 LRF (No. IDC 939) was one of a pair liveried up for the Hanley–Brown Edge–Endon route replacing the double-deckers.

Many of the Pennine vehicles received the First Manchester tomato soup livery ahead of the transfer date of 1 April 2001, such as ECW-bodied Leyland Olympian A733 GFA (No. 7733) seen here at Duckinfield in February 2001. It has received a temporary number by adding a 7 to its former number 733, but is still technically a PMT vehicle at this time.

Some of the Marshall Capital-bodied Dennis Darts transferred from First London worked in the Potteries in London red before being repainted. One such was P128 NLW (No. 40177), seen here on lay over in the old Hanley bus station. These buses had a special number blind made for all Potteries routes.

Following the transfer of the Pennine operation to First Manchester some vehicles returned to the Potteries for further service, but they didn't last long enough to receive another repaint back into red and yellow. Former Crosville ECW-bodied Leyland Olympian KFM 111Y (No. 768) is seen at Newcastle in orange working a No. 34 to Crackley.

Green Line comes to the Potteries! Plaxton Premiere-bodied Volvo B10M R346 GHS
(No. 60041), a recent transfer from First Berkshire, arrives at Newcastle bus station in full
Green Line livery on the X64 Hanley–Shrewsbury service. This was then a joint service with
Arriva Midlands, but had to be given up when the PMT operator's licence was cut in 2004.

Two of the all-Leyland Olympians introduced in 1989 were later transferred to Chester to
operate the X8 from Chester–Banks, which was a joint operation with North Western so they
received the North Western livery. G761 XRE (No. 761) is seen after a repaint at the Adderley
Green paint shop but before the X8 vinyl was applied.

Some of the Leyland Swifts with home-built PMT Knype bodywork were transferred to the Flexi operation so survived in service a little longer in the Potteries. F312 REH (No. 312) has received the attractive blue and white Flexi livery when seen at Newcastle bus station in 2001.

Before buses in the Pennine Blue operation adopted standard red and yellow livery they were painted into a blue and yellow version of the standard livery. YBF 685S (No. 685) has returned to the Potteries and is seen working a No. 23 to Trentham at Stoke still in the blue and yellow livery, but with red zip-style fleet names.

Perhaps the quirkiest buses ever operated by PMT were the five left-hand drive Tecnobus Gulliver nine-seater electric buses operated from Birkenhead depot. S256 AFA (No. MTE 56), the final example of the five, takes a break at Birkenhead Woodside.

Some of the ex-Hong Kong tri-axle, Alexander-bodied Leyland Olympian double-deckers at Pennine started to receive the Barbie 2 livery before the operation transferred to First Manchester on 1 April 2001. K480 EUX (No. 7010) is seen at the Duckinfield garage the week before the transfer, so technically is still a PMT vehicle. These buses never received the tomato soup livery.

The five Plaxton Verde Dennis Lances in the fleet also received the Barbie 2 livery. N867 CEH (No. 60101), seen here in Burslem, was delivered new in the silver, red and yellow livery for the No. 320 Crewe–Hanley route and was later treated to a coat of red and yellow, which it wore briefly before the application of Barbie 2.

Inter-company transfers could always produce interesting arrivals. One such arrival, although very short-lived, was JDZ 2340 (No. 40162), a Wright Handybus-bodied Dennis Dart that was originally in the First London fleet. It is seen at Kidsgrove devoid of blinds, with the route number displayed in the front window on a piece of paper.

Plaxton Pointer-bodied Dennis Dart M960 XVT (No. 960) was one of a batch delivered in the Badgerline era in red and yellow, but has received Barbie 2 and been transferred to the Crosville operation. It is seen here at Chester Bus Interchange.

Only one ECW-bodied Bristol VRT in the First Potteries fleet – and possibly the whole of First Group – ever received the Barbie 2 livery with the fade-out vinyl, and it was already twenty years old when it received it in 2002. GRF 709V (No. 30018) looks resplendent when seen at the Crewe depot shortly afterwards.

Some of the coach-seated Leyland Olympians lost their silver livery and gained the Barbie 2 scheme, such as G758 XRE (No. 30034) seen here at Poolfields on a No. 29 from Keele–Bradeley. These buses were the last double-deckers purchased new by the company in 1989.

Some Leyland Tiger buses with Alexander N-type bodywork joined the fleet from First Manchester, who had obtained them when they acquired the bus operations of Timeline Travel in Manchester, but they had been new to Shearings. G66 RND (No. 60000) is seen at Hanley. Most later became training buses.

A single Volvo B10B with Wright Endurance bodywork, N553 WVR (No. 886) was transferred to First Potteries from First Manchester for the X18 Keele–Hanley–Buxton service, seen here leaving Hanley bus station. It didn't stay long in the fleet and soon returned to First Manchester.

The three Northern Counties Palatine-bodied Dennis Lances (some of the last buses delivered new in red and yellow) eventually received the Barbie 2 livery, but didn't remain in the Potteries for long in this livery before being transferred to Eastern National at Colchester, who operated similar buses. P870 MBF (No. 60104) is seen at Chell Heath before departing for Colchester.

First Potteries also received the Optare Delta-bodied DAF SB220s from Rider York. Some of these ran in service in the former Rider York green livery, but G253 JYG (No. 60017), seen here at Newcastle, received a hybrid livery that was neither Barbie nor Barbie 2. Unlike the PMT examples, which had dual-purpose seats, these had plain bus seating.

Most of the Leyland Lynx single-deckers were repainted by PMT from red and yellow into the Barbie 2 livery before being transferred to Somerset & Avon or Hants & Dorset, but some managed to enter service in the Potteries for a few weeks before the transfer, such as H856 GRE (No. 856), which is seen leaving Hanley for Keele.

The low-height Northern Counties-bodied Leyland Olympians transferred from Yorkshire Rider initially received red and yellow livery and later transferred to Pennine, but were subsequently repainted into the Barbie 2 scheme, such as F160 XYG (No. 30069), which is seen here in Newcastle.

A First Group policy to concentrate small batches of non-standard buses to the same operator saw all the DAF SB220s transferred to First Potteries. Hungarian-built Ikarus Citibus-bodied J426 NCP (No. 60025), seen here in Newcastle, was new to Rider York. All PMT's original DAF SB220s had Optare Delta bodywork.

First Potteries trialled R28 GNW (No. SAD 882), a Plaxton Prestige-bodied DAF SB220 adapted to run on liquid petroleum gas on the Chester Park & Ride. It is seen here on the No. 32 on the Upton Park & Ride, arriving in the city centre in the red, blue and white Park & Ride livery. The tanks for the LPG can be seen on the roof.

The Crosville operation on the Wirral received two batches of Wright Access Ultralow-bodied Scania L113s – some in the new Barbie livery and some in a red, white and blue livery for the Chester Park & Ride. R875 ERE (No. SSS 875) is seen at Prenton in Barbie livery working Merseytravel Smart Route 41D to Mill Park.

The first low-floor buses in the Potteries to wear the First Group corporate Barbie livery for low-floor buses was a batch of nine brand new Scania L113s with Wright Access Ultralow bodywork for Route 6, Kidsgrove–Meir–Blythe Bridge. S819 AEH (No. SSS 819) is seen at Kidsgrove on a No. 6 to Meir Park when new.

The first Optare Solo in the Potteries was W473 SVT (No. 40013), seen here at Newcastle Garage when brand new. These were not the first Solos in the First Potteries fleet as a batch had already been delivered to Chester depot – some in the Flintshire Lynx livery.

A batch of air-conditioned Plaxton Pointer-bodied Dennis Darts were imported into the UK from New World First Bus Hong Kong and allocated to the Potteries fleet. They were converted to single door and issued with UK registrations. S374 SUX (No. 304) is seen at Kidsgrove soon after arriving in 2001.

A handful of the 1989 coach-seated Leyland Olympians received a pink, white and blue livery (based on the new First Bus livery) for the X39 service from Hanley to the popular theme park Alton Towers. G756 XRE (No. 30032) is seen at Newcastle garage shortly after repainting.

Following the abandoning of the Barbie 2 livery for non-low-floor vehicles some went on to receive the now standard Barbie livery. Only one of the Hungarian-built Ikarus Citibus-bodied DAF SB220s ever received this livery – J423 NCP (No. 60022), seen here at the Crewe outstation.

A unique vehicle to arrive in the fleet and destined to have a very short stay was L64 UOU (No. 61212), a Volvo B10M-60 with Plaxton Expressliner bodywork. It was originally used on the National Express network, but was intended to introduce more comfort for passengers on the X1 Derby–Manchester service. It is seen here on the forecourt of Newcastle Garage.

When the number of vehicles that could be operated on the First Potteries operators' licence was cut by the Traffic Commissioners in 2004 some buses were hired in from First Manchester, such as Alexander RV-bodied Volvo Citybus G687 PNS (No. 30372), seen here at Newcastle garage. Being highbridge vehicles they tended to work the Newcastle–Audley routes where there were no low bridges.

Two batches of brand new buses were added to the fleet to increase the age profile after the maintenance issues with the Traffic Commissioners. These were already built and acquired from dealer stock, so were initially white with non-standard interiors. Two Scania Omnicity buses arrived as Nos 65026 and 65027. All-white YN05 HCL (No. 65027) is seen at Stafford.

Also acquired from dealer stock at the same time as the Scania Omnicity buses were seven Wright Solar-bodied Scania L94UB single-deckers – again, in white livery and non-standard red interiors. They also had roller blinds. YN05 HCV (No. 65032) is seen reversing off the stand at Newcastle bus station before receiving fleet livery.

First Potteries have only ever operated one Optare Versa. YJ59 GHH (No. 49001) was owned by Stoke-on-Trent City Council and carried their red, blue and white Cityrider livery with branding for Route 76 Chell Heath–Tunstall–Middleport. It is seen here at Stanfields soon after entering service. This was also the first Optare Versa in any First Group company fleet.

Leyland-bodied Leyland Olympian G753 XRE (No. 65730) is in its twenty-fourth year of service when seen in service at Burslem in February 2013. These veterans were usually confined to schools work, but could appear in normal service at half-term. It was one of ten purchased in 1989, and these were the last new double-deckers purchased by PMT. Some of this batch of buses became the longest serving vehicles in the company's history when finally withdrawn.

September 2011 saw the launch at Stoke Town Hall of the new Gold Service standard for buses on Routes 25 and 26, which saw Wright Eclipse-bodied Volvo B7RLE MX05 CGK (No. 66843) and Scania Omnicity YN05 HCL (No. 65027) receiving the former red and yellow livery with branding for the two routes. A PVR of over twenty buses would have seen many more repaints, but in the event only two more were ever done before the project was quietly abandoned.

Wright Access Floline-bodied Scania L94UB T818 SSF (No. 60171) was the fourth and final repaint into the original red and yellow livery, after which it was quietly abandoned. The buses were later de-branded and from then on tended to appear on any First Potteries route such as seen here at Fegg Hayes on the short-lived diversion of Route 9 via Fegg Hayes Road.

Ten Scania Onmity buses were delivered new in 2006 to upgrade Route 101, Hanley–Stafford. Most received branding for Route 101, with the others in plain Barbie livery as spare vehicles. YN06 WMK (No. 65037) waits at Stafford before returning to Hanley. This bus had a short life and was later withdrawn after accident damage.

Only seven Dennis Darts with Marshall Capital bodywork, V368–74, joined the fleet from Chesterbus when it was purchased in 2007, but other Chesterbus vehicles were hired for a short time. The only one that ever operated in the Potteries was V370 KLG (No. 40170) seen leaving the old Hanley bus station. The other six stayed at Chester and eventually passed to Stagecoach after the sale in 2013.

One of the variety of interesting, older second-hand double-deckers that arrived at First Potteries to replace the original 1989 Olympians on schools services was ex-Strathclyde Buses Volvo Olympian Alexander RL P185 TGD (No. 34285), seen here at rest at the now closed Newcastle garage. It looks smart despite being seventeen years old.

A large batch of second-hand Dennis Darts with Marshall Capital bodywork transferred to the Potteries from First London, with some entering service still in London red livery, but P118 NLW (No. 40165), seen here at Abbey Hulton, has already received a coat of Barbie. A special number blind containing all First Potteries routes was made for these buses.

Another double-decker to arrive in the Potteries to operate Cheshire school contracts was L311 PWR (No. 34311), a Northern Counties Palatine-bodied Volvo Olympian that had been new to Yorkshire Rider but had latterly been working for Eastern National. It occasionally appeared on service work and seen here at Newcastle working a duty on Service 25 Hanley–Keele University.

First Potteries operated many examples of the long Plaxton Pointer Dennis Dart, originating with First Manchester, Yorkshire Rider and Strathclyde Buses all spending time in the Potteries. R335 HYG (No. 40164) originated with Yorkshire Rider and is seen on Beverley Drive Bentilee operating one of the frequent links into Longton from Hanley.

Plaxton Centro-bodied Volvo B7RLE CN57 EFB (No. 66695) looks immaculate after a repaint into First Barbie livery at the Adderley Green Garage paint shop. This bus was new to Veolia in South Wales and came via the Ensignbus dealership. It was being repainted for service in Worcester and never worked in the Potteries.

First Potteries received two batches of the Alexander ALX200-bodied Dennis Dart SLFs brand new, and also acquired a few second-hand examples too, including Former Rider York T372 NUA (No. 40155) seen approaching the old Hanley bus station.

Very few East Lancs-bodied buses have ever worked for First Potteries, but one that did was P859 VUS (No. 40779), an East Lancs Spryte-bodied Dennis Dart seen at Brown Edge Schools on an old Turner's of Brown Edge route. It was new to the Strathclyde Buses low-cost GCT unit in Glasgow.

Caetano Nimbus-bodied Dennis Dart Y353 AUY (No. 42353), seen here at Chell Heath, was one of five buses initially leased to First Midland Red for the Worcester City Park & Ride services. Subsequently purchased by Midland Red, it was one of three later transferred to First Potteries for further service.

Plaxton Mini Pointer Dennis Dart S766 RNE (No. 40003) was one of a pair to transfer from First Manchester to the Potteries. It had been new to Springfield Coachways for its Easy Link services in Wigan, which were later purchased by First Manchester. The other one of the pair worked from Chester for Crosville.

UVG Urbanstar-bodied Dennis Dart P750 XUS (No. 40745), seen here arriving at Abbey Hulton on a No. 5 from Hanley, was one of three examples to arrive in the Potteries for further service. It was new to Kelvin Scottish and initially used in competition against Stagecoach on the former A1 service routes on the Clyde Coast in Ayrshire.

Wright Access Floline-bodied Scania L94UB S572 TPW (No. 65572), seen here at Fegg Hayes, was one of a handful of buses purchased for spares by First Potteries from storage at Northampton garage after the closure of the First Northampton business. They proved to be in better condition than the buses they were due to provide spares for, however, so were promptly put back in service.

First Potteries received a number of Alexander ALX400-bodied Volvo B7TL double-deckers from Leicester, including W217 XBD (No. 32057), seen here at Kidsgrove. Despite their age these would be the newest double-deckers in the fleet. None of these ever received the refreshed Olympia livery or the later fuschia front scheme.

A more interesting arrival from First Northampton was Alexander-bodied Volvo Citybus K125 URP (No. 38125), which was the first highbridge bus to enter the fleet since the ex-Midland Red Fleetlines in 1977. It was kept at Newcastle garage and tended to stay on Cheshire school routes. It was fully refurbished by First Potteries and received a repaint into Barbie livery. It carried an original Northampton destination blind to the end.

First Potteries eventually received all of the Alexander Dennis Enviro 300 buses that were new to First Worcester, apart from the three transferred to Diamond in 2013 following the sale of the Kidderminster and Redditch depots. The first to arrive was Transbus VX53 VJV (No. 67601), seen here at Chell Heath. Most arrived in the original Barbie livery, and some were never repainted before they were withdrawn.

The arrival of the first Volvo B7TL double-deckers with Wright Eclipse Gemini bodywork from First Leicester enabled the last of the elderly non-low-floor double-deckers to be withdrawn, and this model would eventually become the standard double-decker in the fleet. KP54 LAE (No. 32633) is seen here at Poolfields.

Volvo Olympian Northern Counties Palatine 2 P658 UFB (No. 34158), seen here at Kidsgrove, was one of the eldest buses in the country to receive the new, refreshed First Olympia livery. It was new to First Bristol and came to First Potteries to replace the 1989 Olympians, primarily on Cheshire school routes.

Another Volvo Olympian to join the fleet around the same time was ex-Strathclyde Buses P186 TGD (No. 32486), this time with Alexander bodywork. This was the only one of the three examples at First Potteries that would receive the Olympia livery and is seen parked at the now closed Newcastle garage.

Caetano Nimbus-bodied Dennis Dart EU06 KDK (No. 43877), seen here at Newcastle bus station, was the only short wheelbase Dennis Dart with bodywork by this bodybuilder to work in the Potteries. New to S. M. Coaches at Harlow, it worked for many small independent operators around the country before being sold to Ensignbus and subsequent purchase by First Group.

Short-lived competition in early 2014 with Bakerbus on its Hanley-Bentilee routes saw First Potteries add yellow Bee Buzz brandings to some of the Caetano-bodied Dennis Darts for Routes 1 and 2 to Bentilee. In typical Potteries fashion, LK03 LNV (No. 41499) is off route on a No. 21 at Hanford. Bakers didn't stay on the route long, so the branding on these buses was soon removed. The bus was new to First London.

MX56 HYO (No. 43875), seen here at Mill Hill, was one of two Alexander Dennis Mini Pointer Darts to arrive in the First Potteries fleet from the large batch of modern second-hand buses purchased by First Group from the Ensignbus dealership. It was new to National Car Parks but had latterly operated for Centrebus at Leicester.

The only Optare Solo from the home fleet to receive the refreshed Olympia livery was W477 SVT (No. 40018), seen at Kidsgrove King Street on the long, withdrawn No. 99A from Kidsgrove to Newcastle via Tunstall and Newchapel.

A few of the Wright Eclipse Urban-bodied Volvo B7RLE single-deckers received the Olympia livery, as seen on MX05 CFY (No. 66839) leaving Newcastle bus station. This bus was among a batch that were transferred from First Manchester where they were replaced by Wright Gemini-bodied Volvo B7 double-deckers.

Not many of the numerous Wright-bodied Scanias in the First Potteries fleet received the Olympia livery, but S105 TNB (No. 60128), seen here at Brookwood Drive, Meir, on the No. 26 from Newcastle–Hanley, was one of those that did. This bus was new to First Manchester.

Dennis Dart SLF R979 NVT (No. 40137) was new to the Crosville depot at Birkenhead. Seen here at Mill Hill was one of the first buses delivered new in the standard Barbie livery in the First Potteries fleet. It later transferred from the Wirral to the Potteries and was the only one to receive the refreshed Olympia livery.

Some of the Scania Omnicitys allocated to the No. 101 Hanley–Stafford route since brand new in 2006 started to receive the refreshed Olympia livery, but lost their route branding in the process. YN06 WMF (No. 65034) arrives at Kidsgrove on a No. 7 for Hanley. Those that were repainted didn't last long in this livery before receiving the fuchsia front scheme.

A batch of five 2007 Wright Eclipse Gemini-bodied Volvo B9TL double-deckers transferred from Norwich in the refreshed Olympia livery. AU07 DXS (No. 37156) is seen at Mill Hill shortly after arriving in the Potteries. Some of these buses have amassed high mileages as they used to work on the lengthy X1 Excel between Norwich and Peterborough.

One of the first recipients of the new Cherry Route red front livery for the Nos 3 and 4 group of routes was Wright Eclipse Urban-bodied Volvo B7RLE KV02 VVN (No. 66311), seen at the now closed Newcastle garage. First Potteries received a batch of these buses from Leicester to update the age profile of its fleet, with most being repainted into this livery.

The five Scania Omnicity buses YN04 YJC-G (Nos 65001–5) received the interurban mauve front livery with branding for the No. 18 Hanley–Leek–Haregate as seen on YN04 YJG (No. 65005) at Endon. These buses were later replaced by newer models from First Essex and rebranded as the Leek Link.

Two ex-West Yorkshire Optare Solos received this attractive blue front livery for Route 38, Hanley–Birches Head circular. W327 DWX (No. 50296) is seen at Birches Head. This route would be abandoned by First Potteries a few years later, with the two buses departing the fleet soon afterwards.

Only one Optare Solo received the all-routes spare bus mauve front livery. It was X299 FFA (No. 40029), seen here waiting time at Bradeley on a No. 9 to Hanley – another route that would later be abandoned by First Potteries during the years of contraction.

The first new buses for First Potteries for many years were a batch of ten door-forward versions of the Wright Streetlite. They were delivered in 2014 with the raspberry front livery for the six group of routes from Hanley to Meir and Blythe Bridge. SN64 CGE (No. 63171) is seen leaving Longton bus station when brand new.

Pending the delivery of the tenth Wright Streetlite, which was to be a Euro 6 version, former Wright demonstrator DRZ 9713 (No. 63180) worked for First Potteries but never received any fleet names and had a different type of destination display. It is seen here at Meir Square. This bus had previously worked for Bus Eireann in Ireland as a demonstrator.

The tenth and final Wright Streetlite finally arrived in spring 2015 and received the registration 'SN15 ABF' (No. 66250). It is seen at Adderley Green depot undergoing tests before entering service. It didn't stay long in the Potteries, however, being transferring to First Leicester soon afterwards.

Following the decision to abandon the different colour fronts livery and make the raspberry front (now renamed fuchsia) the future standard, repaints in this livery commenced. Optare Solo CN06 BXH (No. 53155), seen here at Chell, was one of the first to be done. It was one of only two Solos ever to receive this livery at First Potteries.

In autumn 2015, Caetano Nimbus-bodied Dennis Dart LK53 LDZ (No. 41540) received a colourful vinyl wrap for the Stoke-on-Trent *Evening Sentinel*, the local evening newspaper, in a blue and purple livery seen here at Blurton working a No. 23 to Hanley. This bus was new to First London as a dual-door bus.

Also in autumn 2015, Scania Omnicity YN06 WMO (No. 65040) also received a vinyl wrap advertising for the local newspaper, the *Evening Sentinel*, this time in an orange and pink livery. It tended to work on the No. 10 Hanley–Stafford route and is seen here at Trent Vale shortly after it was applied.

More new buses were delivered to First Potteries in the autumn of 2016; this time ten Alexander Dennis Enviro 200MMC single-deckers arrived for Routes 21 and 23. YX66 WFL (No. 67153) passes through Fenton on a No. 23 to Newstead shortly afterwards.

Volvo B7TL Wright Eclipse Gemini KP54 LAO (No. 32634) was repainted into the pre-NBC dark red and cream PMT livery for the First Potteries 2016 Adderley Green depot open day, and looks resplendent working a No. 25 from Hanley at Keele University shortly afterwards.

The other heritage repaint launched at the 2016 First Potteries Adderley Green depot open day was Volvo B7TL Wright Eclipse Gemini YN06 UPZ (No. 37145), which received the silver, red and yellow livery previously used on the Leyland Olympians used on the No. 320 Hanley–Crewe route. The Gemini is seen at the Royal Stoke University Hospital.

Volvo B7TL Wright Eclipse Gemini KP54 KBK (No. 32648) arrives at Keele University in the fuchsia front livery and with branding for the busy No. 25 Hanley–Stoke Station–Keele University route. This bus came to First Potteries from First Leicester. Ten Geminis carry this branding for this busy student route.

Only one Alexander Dennis Enviro 300 ever ran in service in the Potteries in the Olympia livery. Ex-First Worcester FN08 AZZ (No. 67665) passes through Butt Lane on a No. 4A to Hanley. This bus was new to Premiere Travel Nottingham and came to First Group via the Ensignbus dealership.

Training buses have always been an important member of the bus fleet, usually being a recently retired vehicle converted for the new role. Here, former First Manchester Wright Endurance-bodied Volvo B10B N521 WVR (No. 60316) waits for its next trainee at Adderley Green garage.

Towards the end of 2018, Scania Omnicity YN05 HCL (No. 65027) was repainted out of the red and yellow heritage livery into the original red and cream PMT livery with gold numerals. It is seen here looking immaculate at Poolfields on a No. 25 to Keele University.

First Worcester transferred two short Wright Streetlites to First Potteries in early 2019. Both arrived in the original Olympia livery, but soon received a repaint into the fuchsia front livery. SN64 CFY (No. 47519) is seen a Newchapel soon after arriving in the Potteries.

All the Alexander Dennis Enviro 300s new to First Worcester eventually joined the First Potteries fleet, but FN08 AZZ (No. 67665) was new to Premiere Nottingham and came via the Ensign Bus dealership. It received branding for Bentilee–Hanley in 2019 and is seen waiting time at Newcastle before returning to Hanley via Bentilee.

The Scania Omnicity buses used on the No. 101 Hanley–Stafford route didn't last long in the Olympia livery and soon received the fuchsia front livery with branding for the No. 101 route. YN06 WME (No. 65033) is seen at Newcastle. This livery, too, was short-lived and was later replaced by the Knotty scheme.

The final Alexander Dennis Enviro 300 to arrive from First Worcester was the newest and differed from the rest by having the revised front end and gasket glazing. PT59 JPT (No. 65999) was new to Manchester independent JP Travel and still carries its private plate. It is seen in Newcastle in April 2019 shortly after entering service after a repaint.

WX05 UAJ (No. 42552) was one of three mini-Pointer Darts transferred in from First Somerset and Avon and later received the fuchsia front livery to work alongside the Enviro 200 MMC buses on Routes 21 and 23, but subsequent service reductions saw them work on other routes like the No. 99 seen here at Chell Heath in August 2019.

An elderly arrival into the First Potteries fleet in early 2019 was Wright Solar-bodied Scania L94UB YS03 ZKM (No. 65692), which could usually be found working Bradeley–Tunstall shorts during the roadworks at Porthill that year. It didn't last long and was withdrawn by 2020.

After accident damage Wright Solar-bodied Scania L94UB YN05 HCV (No. 65732) received a partial repaint, with the red front repainted fuchsia. This was the only one of these buses to receive the fuchsia front livery, and is seen here at Kidsgrove library on a No. 3A to Hanley.

Three Alexander Dennis Enviro 200 Darts were transferred from First Worcester in spring 2019. Two were repainted before entering service, but MX10 DXU (No. 44515) entered service in the former Olympia livery and is seen at Abbey Hulton. This bus was new to Premiere Nottingham but purchased by First Group from Ensign Bus.

Another of the ex-Worcester Enviro 200s was DK57 SPZ (No. 44511), which received the fuchsia front livery before entering service, is seen dropping off a passenger at Chell Heath in autumn 2019. The bus was new to Townlynx Holywell and was one of the large batch of modern second-hand buses that First Group purchased from Ensignbus.

Four of the ex-First Essex Scania Omnicity buses acquired in March 2019 were refurbished, repainted into a three-tone green livery and branded as the Leek Link for Route 18, Hanley–Leek. YN06 TDX (No. 65031) waits at Sneyd Green after having just recently entered service in March 2020.

Seven of the Scania Omnicity buses that have been used on the No. 101 Hanley–Stafford route since new in 2006 were also refurbished in 2020, being repainted into a stunning two-tone purple livery and rebranded as the Knotty. YN06 WMG (No. 65035) arrived in Newcastle in August 2020.

The black and grey-liveried Scania Omnicity spare buses, intended to work on the Leek Link, Knotty and Kingfisher routes when their own buses are unavailable, occasionally appear on other routes. YN06 TDZ (No. 65032) arrives at Kidsgrove on a No. 7 for Hanley. This bus was also new to First Essex.

Instead of working between Hanley and Uttoxeter, the turquoise and orange Kingfisher-branded, Wright Gemini-bodied Volvo B9TL double-deckers tended to be allocated to the busier routes during the Covid-19 pandemic during the summer of 2020 due to their greater capacity. AU07 DXX (No. 37160) waits time at Kidsgrove while working a No. 3A from Butt Lane to Hanley.

During the Covid-19 pandemic reduced capacity was introduced on buses to comply with new social distancing regulations. This resulted in a new 'Bus Full' destination being displayed on the destination blinds, as seen on ex-First Manchester Wright Streetlite SK63 KGA (No. 63113) at Whitehill in July 2020 working a No. 7 to Hanley.

The Leek Link-branded Scania Omnicity buses started to appear on other routes during the Covid-19 pandemic as a reduced service to Leek, coupled with extra buses being required on other routes due to reduced capacity, made cameo appearances commonplace. Ex-First Essex YN06 TDV (No. 65030) waits in Sandyford with a short working on Route 3 to Hanley in September 2020.

In early 2020, Alexander Dennis Enviro 200 MMC YY66 PXP (No. 67159), seen here at Newcastle bus station, received lettering stating that First Potteries was proud to have been part of the Potteries since 1898. It also received all the six different fleet names ever carried in that time above the windows in gold.

Preserved PMT Leyland Olympian G759 XRE (No. 759) looks immaculate in NBC poppy red when seen parked outside Newcastle garage in June 2017, but is not quite what it seems. The bus was delivered after the NBC sale in silver, red and yellow livery, later receiving the First Barbie livery, so never wore poppy red in service with PMT. On withdrawal it was sold for preservation and later passed to a dance troupe and was painted poppy red. It then passed back into preservation again before being exported to the USA.

In early 2021 a batch of 2006-registered Volvo B7RLE single-deckers arrived in the Potteries to start replacing the Alexander Dennis Enviro 300s. New to First Manchester, these buses then passed on hire to Diamond following the sale of Bolton depot. On their return to First Group they were allocated to First Potteries. MV06 CZJ (No. 69172) is seen at Chell Heath shortly after entering service with First Potteries in January 2021.